READ AND SHARE™

The Story of Easter

This book is for:

From:

Date:

Published in Nashville, Tennessee, by Thomas Nelson. Thomas Nelson is a trademark of Thomas Nelson, Inc.

Thomas Nelson, Inc., books may be purchased in bulk for educational, business, fund-raising, or sales promotional use. For information, please e-mail SpecialMarkets@ThomasNelson.com.

Story based on The Holy Bible, International Children's Bible®, copyright © 1986, 1988, 1999, 2005 by Thomas Nelson, Inc.

Story retold by Gwen Ellis.
Illustrated by Steve Smallman.

Library of Congress Cataloging-in-Publication Data
Ellis, Gwen.
The story of Easter : read and share / story retold by Gwen Ellis ; illustrated by Steve Smallman.
        p. cm.
   ISBN 978-1-4003-0855-2 (hardback : alk. paper) 1. Holy Week—Juvenile literature. 2. Easter—Juvenile literature. 3. Jesus Christ—Passion—Juvenile literature. 4. Jesus Christ—Appearances—Juvenile literature.
I. Smallman, Steve. II. Title.
   BT414.E45 2007
   232.9'7—c22

                                                                                                    2007029483

Printed in China
07 08 09 10 11 MT 5 4 3 2

READ AND SHARE™

The Story of Easter

Retold by
Gwen Ellis

Illustrated by Steve Smallman

THOMAS NELSON
Since 1798

NASHVILLE   DALLAS   MEXICO CITY   RIO DE JANEIRO   BEIJING

Jesus Borrows a Donkey

Luke 19:28–35

The first Passover happened when God's people left Egypt long ago. After that, God's people celebrated Passover every year. One year Jesus and His closest followers went to Jerusalem to celebrate Passover.

Before they got there, Jesus said to His followers, "Go into town and find a young donkey colt. Untie it and bring it to Me. If anyone asks where you are taking it, say, 'The Master needs it.'" When the men got back with the donkey colt, they spread their coats on its back. Jesus climbed on the colt.

Why do you suppose Jesus needed that donkey colt?

Jesus Rides Like a King

Luke 19:36–38; John 12:12–16

The donkey started to clippity-clop through the town. People came running. They threw their coats down for the donkey to walk on. They took palm branches and waved them in the air. "Praise God!" they shouted.

Some of them remembered the scriptures that said, "Your king is coming . . . sitting on the colt of a donkey."

Why do you suppose they laid their coats down for the donkey to walk on?
Did they think Jesus was a king?

The First Lord's Supper

Matthew 26:26–29; 1 Corinthians 11:23–25;
Luke 22:18; Mark 14:25

While Jesus and His closest followers were eating the Passover dinner, Jesus took some bread and thanked God for it. He broke the bread apart and said, "Take this bread and eat it. Do this to remember Me."

Next He took a cup and said, "When you drink this juice of the grape, remember Me." Jesus knew this was His last meal with His followers because He was about to be killed. He wanted His followers to always remember Him.

Today in church we still eat bread and drink the juice of the grape to remember Jesus. We call this time of remembering *Communion* or *The Lord's Supper*.

Jesus Prays for Help

Matthew 26:36–40; Mark 14:32–42; Luke 22:39–46

Jesus and His followers went straight from dinner to a quiet garden. Jesus wanted to pray and ask God to make Him strong for what was about to happen. He took three of His closest followers— Peter, James, and John—apart from the others. Jesus asked them to wait and pray.

He went a little farther into the garden to pray by Himself. It was very late, and the three men were very tired. They couldn't keep their eyes open to pray. Soon they were asleep. Jesus woke them twice, but they went back to sleep each time.

When we have tough things ahead of us, we need to pray and ask God to help us.

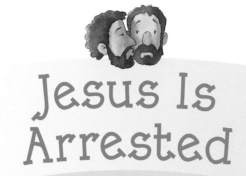

Jesus Is Arrested

Matthew 26:45–56; Luke 22:45–51;
John 18:10–11

The third time Jesus woke His followers,
He said, "We must go. Here comes the man
who has turned against Me." Just then a big
crowd carrying torches and clubs came into
the garden. Judas, one of Jesus' followers, was
with them. He kissed Jesus on the cheek. It
was a signal to the guards to arrest Jesus.

Peter pulled out his sword and cut off the ear of one guard. Jesus told Peter to put the sword away. Then He healed the guard's ear.

You might think the crowd would let Jesus go after He healed the man's ear. Well, they didn't. They arrested Him and took Him away.

Pilate Questions Jesus

Luke 22:52–23:25

Lots of people loved Jesus, but there were many who didn't like Him at all. After Jesus was captured in the garden, He was taken to the house of the high priest, then to Pilate, the Roman governor of Judea.

All night the rulers asked Jesus if He was God's Son. They did not believe that He was. Finally Pilate said that he didn't think Jesus was guilty. But the people who hated Jesus kept yelling until Pilate decided that Jesus had to die on a cross.

Jesus told everyone that He was God's Son, and that made some people very angry. But even if they didn't believe it, He was still God's Son.

Jesus Is Killed on a Cross

Matthew 27:27–40; Mark 15:25–27

Pilate's soldiers took Jesus and put a crown of thorns on His head and made fun of Him. Then they led Jesus out of the city to a place called Golgotha to be killed on a cross.

At nine o'clock in the morning, the soldiers nailed Jesus to the cross. They also put two robbers beside Jesus, one on the right and one on the left.

The day God's Son died on the cross was a sad day. But God had a wonderful plan. Keep reading and you'll see what it was.

A Dark Day

Matthew 27:45–54; Luke 23:44–49; Hebrews 9

While Jesus was on the cross, the land became dark from noon until three o'clock. Then Jesus died, and there was a big earthquake.

When the earth shook, the thick curtain in the Temple between the Holy Place and the Most Holy Place ripped from top to bottom. Now people could see inside the Most Holy Place. Before, only the High Priest got to see inside. When the soldiers at the cross saw what happened when Jesus died, they knew He really was the Son of God.

Jesus died because He loved us. He died so that our sins could be forgiven. Let's tell Him right now that we love Him for what He did on the cross.

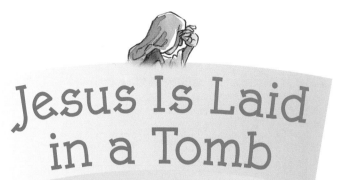

Jesus Is Laid in a Tomb

Luke 23:50–56; Matthew 27: 62–66
John 19: 38–42

A rich man, named Joseph, of Arimathea, had a new tomb where he had planned to be buried. He took Jesus' body from the cross and put it in his own empty tomb.

Joseph and Jesus' friends wrapped His body in strips of linen and laid it carefully in the tomb. A huge stone was rolled in front of the door. Roman soldiers came to guard the tomb. They sealed the stone in a way that would show if anyone tried to move it.

Everyone thought that since Jesus was dead, they would never see Him again. They were in for a big surprise!

A Big Surprise

Matthew 28:1–10

The day after Jesus was buried was a holy day, so His friends had to stay home. Then, very early on Sunday morning, the first day of the week, some women went to the tomb. It was the third day since Jesus died.

When the women got there, they couldn't believe their eyes. The stone had been rolled away! An angel of God was sitting on the stone! The soldiers were so frightened, they were like dead men.

How do you think the women at the tomb felt when they saw the angel?

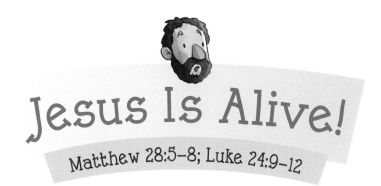

Jesus Is Alive!

Matthew 28:5–8; Luke 24:9–12

The angel said, "Don't be afraid. Jesus is alive." Those women were as happy as they could be! They ran to find other friends of Jesus.

Some of Jesus' friends didn't believe what the women said. But everything the women had said was true. Jesus was alive! He had risen from death.

Jesus promised He would come back to life . . . and He did. Jesus is alive today and will be forever. How long is forever?

Jesus Appears to a Room Full of Friends

Luke 24:33–49

One night Jesus appeared in a room where many of His friends were gathered. He told them to tell their family and friends and neighbors and even strangers that He is alive.

He told them to share everything He had taught them. They were to tell the people in Jerusalem first, but then they were to tell people everywhere. Jesus told them to wait in Jerusalem until God sent them a special gift of power from heaven.

Whom do you know that would like to hear all about Jesus' love?

Jesus Goes to Heaven

Luke 24:50–53; Acts 1:6–11

Jesus led His friends a little way out of town. Jesus prayed for His friends, and while He was praying, He started to rise up into heaven. Then a cloud hid Him from His friends.

As everyone was standing there staring up into heaven, two angels appeared beside them and said, "Jesus has been taken away from you and into heaven. He will come back in the clouds, just like He went away."

We are still waiting for the angels' promise to happen. Jesus will come back someday.

Can You Retell the Story?

The pictures on this page and the next pages are all mixed up. Do you remember what happened first? Point to the pictures in the correct order and retell the story.